ARCHANGELOLOGY MARY MAGDALENE FEMININE DIVINE

IF YOU CALL THEM THEY WILL COME

ARCHANGELOLOGY BOOK SERIES
BOOK 21

KIM CALDWELL

A Division of Archangelology LLC

https://archangelology.com

This publication is designed to provide competent and reliable information regarding the subject matter covered. However, it is sold with the understanding that the author and publisher are not engaged in rendering medical and healthcare or any advice. Archangelology LLC, Together Publishing and all offerings are for entertainment purpose only. If you need medical, financial or any kind of help please consult a qualified professional. This is an energy book there is no advice intended or given.

Introduction Editing and enhancement Rachel Caldwell

Book Editing Grammarly

ISBN: 978-1-947284-45-6

Book Cover Picture Nicola Zalewski

Cover design Kim Caldwell

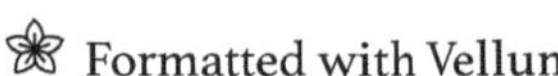
Formatted with Vellum

Here, the Feminine Divine expresses as we connect to our Heart Center; Archangel Haniel will assist with this while we go into our Highest Holy Self; Archangel Raziel will help us connect to this, as we see the infinity sign, which looks like an 8 connecting the Heart and Mind, bringing them together online in a Powerful way that helps them work Together. Bringing the Heart and mind Together more consciously, on purpose, will bring in more insight, new blessings, and new ways of experiencing the Divine Feminine Power in our lives. As all of this is happening, we connect deeply and drop our grounding cord into Mother Earth; Archangel Sandalphon will be assisting with this. As we connect with the nurturing, supportive energies of Mother Earth, while we are heart-centered and in our higher self, our "Secret Smile Blossoms", that knowing of who we are, the understanding of our connection to that part of us that is the Feminine Divine.

The Feminine Divine is flowing. intuitive, brilliant, and who better to guide us on this journey than Mary Magdalene and the Feminine Form of the Archangels? The Feminine Divine knows how to Receive, and this will enable us to Receive more of the blessings that we deserve in our lives. As we spend more time connected in our Feminine Divine Energy through this process that brings forth our "Secret Smile", we will ultimately feel more "Heaven on Earth" for ourselves and those around us. Our "Secret Smile" is a practice that we may play with often when we are in the mood, with joy in our hearts. We want to be very easy on ourselves about this and enlist the help of Mary Magdalene, the Feminine Archangels, and our Higher Self to ease and guide this process. Feel the Trinity 3 energy in the concepts above.

The Feminine Divine is rising, and this will benefit the Entire World. May all beings be happy and free. May this practice of your Secret Smile bring you great Alignment, Prosperity, Joy, and Blessings.

Each time in your book that you see the "Secret Smile" process signified by the 8 stars ********, it is time to take a deep breath and practice your "Secret Smile" with Mary Magdalene and your Feminine Archangels.

As you practice your "Secret Smile", this will become more beneficial, consistent, and flowing. And you will notice how it brings you more into your Feminine Divine Power, a Power that feels like Alignment, Peace, and Home.

The Feminine Divine feels like a nurturing, secure Power. You may quietly bring this practice of your Secret Smile into any area of your life that you would like to enhance, upgrade, or enjoy more. With patience and practice of your "Secret Smile", you can expect favorable results. Your secret smile, Feminine Divine, with your Heart activated and your connection to higher self, while grounded to Mother Earth, see and feel a beautiful Violet Flame circle all around you, transmuting, healing, and upgrading the entire process; Archangel Zadkiel will stand with you for this. Play with this process, make it your own, do what is most comfortable for you. As always, your opinion comes first; what feels best to you is the most important.

The Divine Feminine is Relaxed and slows to Feel, Breathe, Allow, and ultimately

Align. There is no hurry; there is no rush, as there is always Enough, as Goddess Mother Earth demonstrates Feminine Flowing of Abundance.

Feminine Divine does not recognize 'lost chances', as there is always another opportunity to experience this ever-flowing supply, the Knowing of Divine Connection to all that is, and the "Secret Smile" that accompanies this magical state of being.

Your Divine Feminine is eternal; it makes no difference whether you are male or female. This Divine intelligence flows through us all. This infinite, creative, beautiful, allowing Essence that creates life on the earth, that brings so many blessings to all who Embrace the Divine Feminine. It does not matter your age; Divine Intelligence and magnetism with the Sacred Feminine shine through, allowing this imagination creation with Mary Magdalene and the Feminine Archangels to connect you and remind you of your Divine Feminine Power.

The Feminine Divine is fiercely protective of Freedom, Equality, and anything else that says Divine Intelligence to you. The Archangelology Series, with the help of Mary Magdalene, steps up to help bring in the Feminine Divine as well. Here, in all their Glory, Mary Magdalene and the Feminine Archangels reveal and revel in their Feminine Form.

Focusing our heart-centered "Secret Smile" brings a fresh perspective to our world because it is so different from human "trying" to "fix". One of the Divine Feminine messages is that we do not fix anything; we Align. We Align with that still, deep part of us that is Infinite Intelligence, the Powerful Feminine Divine.

If one observes "unacceptable behaviors," the Divine Feminine "Secret Smile" steps in to help Melt and Transmute them through the Power of Observation with more grace and ease. May this wisdom bring more Freedom, Equality, Peace, and Blessings. May women around the world be safe and Blessed. May the men who support women and the Feminine Divine Be Blessed. May the Divine Feminine and Divine Masculine dance Together in a way that brings new peace, blessings and understanding. May Mary Magdalene, the Feminine Archangels, the Saints, and the Enlightened Beings continue to help and guide us. May we see more Heaven on Earth.

Someone may find the path to alignment in many ways; the one we will be following today is that of the Feminine Divine. We will now spend some time focusing on that Divine Feminine alignment to Source, with the intention of seeing the Divine Feminine aspect of us as Powerful, Creative, and a Force for good to be respected—that ability to get still and quiet and connect to Infinite Intelligence, your Higher Self.

That Divine Feminine Intuition that leads us to desired places that anyone may develop with practice and patience. Honoring that place within every one of us is the intention of this Mary Magdalene, flowing and flowing us to a bright and brilliant now with the Power of the Feminine Divine and our unparalleled imagination, the Creative Force.

The Archangels chose this moment to come and appear to us in their Feminine

Form, as we see that Divine Feminine facet of us as Powerful, Worthy, and Effective. More often, it will emerge in delightful new ways we only imagined. Spend time now and here with Mary Magdalene, the Divine Feminine Force, and your Archangels to forge a path with Love, Peace, Light, and Intuition. These emerging qualities will please and delight your life, so get ready to soar with the Feminine Archangels to new Heights.

Let your imagination be free and creative with your Divine Feminine Archangels. Let all the creative energies flow as you envision your Magnificent Feminine Archangel team working for you in any area you want. See and feel Your Archangels as Empowered, Glowing, and adorned in Regal costumes that dazzle your Spirit. Know that these Radiant Beings are here for you. We imagine and focus on the Feminine Divine part of us as powerful subconscious shifts take place for our benefit. This imagination creation empowers a dormant strength that, when tapped into, reveals our potential and the Universe in new and exciting ways; this quiet stillness holds Unimaginable Divine Power that we ignite. Let your Imagination Shimmer and Shine with Mary Magdalene and the Divine Feminine Archangels. You may want to imagine your Feminine Divine Archangel Power removing non-beneficial energies with elegance and ease, creating Golden, vast spaces for more Blessings.

The audio to this book has been available on archangelologydotcom for years. I did not complete this matching book until the start of 2026, when the Chinese Astralogical year of the Fire Horse began. This year is powerful, and I invite you to do your own research on the Fire Horse year. I found the whole alignment fascinating, as these Divine New Feminine Energies emerged at such an auspicious time. Like this book was waiting for this year to "Be Born". This Mary Magdalene book and matching audio contain a Pegasus, which, as you know, is another version of the graceful horse energy. So please know, as you spend time visualising your Fire Pegasus with your Archangels, you are creating magick on new divine levels.

As you play with this new game, many ideas will come to Mind. Remember to connect the Mind with your Heart. As you enlist this Divine Intelligence that we all have access to, many new ideas of how your Feminine Archangels may help and play with you will evolve.

King Solomon was known for working very successfully with the Goddess Energy, so you are in good company for bringing the Divine Feminine Energy into your life.

May you always be Blessed and Prospered by your Divine Feminine Energies.

Kim Caldwell

2

SECRET SMILE ENERGY RESET ACTIVATION PROCESS

"Inner Sweet Smile" Process and Activation

Please be patient with this process and allow it to flow into and help you with all aspects of your life. This is your true nature and thus your Power. Use it with great confidence and wisdom as you are naturally able to. Claim your birthright for this Divine Feminine Power. Let it bring you all the Blessings. Be easy with this and open to this process becoming more.

. . .

When the 8 stars for your ********Inner Sweet Smile ******** appear, it is time to practice your Sweet Smile Process.

******** "Inner Sweet Smile" Activation. Please take this moment to Pause. Take a deep, relaxing breath, and visualize Mary Magdalene standing before you. Allow her beautiful, Divine Feminine Energy to infuse you with deep Peace as Mary Magdalene guides you to activate your heart center. Call Archangel Haniel to assist while you take as much time as needed to feel all the Love in your Heart radiating in and around you. Breathe in deep Love, as you breathe out, fill your space up with all this Divine Love. Breathe Love in and out, and when ready, connect with your higher self. Archangel Raziel, the great Archangel of wisdom, stands beside you to help you feel your Higher Self coming online. Be easy on yourself, and know that your intentions for connecting with your Higher Self are making it happen. Feel as your Heart and Mind sync and align

Together. Now, when ready, send your grounding cord down into Mother Earth and feel securely connected. Archangel Sandalphon stands beside you, helping you connect to Mother Earth now. Take your time, and when ready, feel your Violet Flame form a circle around you to establish healthy transmutative boundaries. Allow any non-beneficial or dense energies transmute to Love, Light, and Blessings. Archangel Zadkiel stands on your borders, helping you to run your Violet Flame in this Divine Feminine Circle. Hold this feeling as long as desired and allow your imaginative Feminine Energies to infuse your experience with Power and Peace. Feel and immerse yourself in this Divine Feminine Flow now.********

Understand that repetition is a great teacher, and this is why you will see this process often in this book. As you get familiar with this process and practice it consistently, it will happen more quickly and easily, and in time, it will just become a lovely, beneficial habit.

Again, be patient with this process and easy on yourself. There is no hurry, and this practice is a blessing, so please enjoy it. Just practicing this will bring about great blessings. Have faith. Archangels, please assist with this.

Remember to call your Archangels frequently to help you with this Secret Smile process, and the more you practice, the better you flow at activating it. Be assured that as you practice activating your secret smile, you are holding a Divine Frequency for your Empowerment and allowing such blessings by being you and radiating this Divine Feminine Signal. ********

Spend Divine Time going to a fantastic, happy place with your Archangels, Mary Magdalene, and your team to a peaceful, relaxing home in your Heart and imagination.

Now is the perfect opportunity to practice that still Magical Feminine Divine place in you and radiate it into your world. Practice this often, and do so away from your book if inspired as well. Let this become a beneficial habit. As they say, "our habits make us who we are," and this habit will bring you right into your Feminine Divine Wisdom and Empowerment. Let us cultivate the habit of imagining incredible blessings, radiating them into your life for more Peace, Self-Love, Well-Being, and Fortune. May Mary Magdalene and the Archangels assist you in this endeavor for the highest good of all involved. May this practice bring you Bright Blessings. Please remember this imagination practice is supposed to be fun. Please take a break and play when it does not feel like ease and joy.

A word about connecting to your higher self: once we become aware of the benefits of connecting to our higher self and start connecting, the question will arise: how do I connect, and once I try, am I doing this right?

Each person had the ability and birthright to connect to that part of them that is Divine. And each person will do this process in their own way. As you set intentions and call to connect with your higher self, it will naturally happen, like breathing. The more you practice, the better it will feel.

Try to let your Heart Guide this process with Mary Magdalene and your Archangels, and not overthink it. You are a wise ancient spiritual being, and you have got this. Have faith and have fun with it.

3

THE POWER TO TRANSMUTE

It has been explained to me on many occasions that energy is neither good nor bad; it is all energy. When a person is going through challenges, this feels harder to comprehend, let alone accept. Yet the message kept finding me, and in the same-ish words. The best wisdom that came through is to focus on the transmutation of energy. At least setting the intention. So I present to you that humans can transmute energy into more of what they desire. And that the Feminine Divine Secret Smile is a great way to do this transmutation. Set intentions that the Archangels, Saints, and Secret Smile help transmute any non- beneficial energy to Blessings. Play with this process, and as always, do what is best for you. Setting these intentions is a great place to start and see where the Golden Path takes you.

4

ABOUT THE SERIES

"Logic will get you from point A to B. Imagination will take you everywhere."--Einstein

This Archangelology book and the entire series aim to lift the reader one step at a time. You may read this piece anytime you desire Upliftment and want to feel good now, never underestimate the power of feeling good for creating more of what you want.

Choose this or any of the other Archangelology Books or Matching Audios to read or listen to for at least 44 nights and raise your vibration consistently for an Uplifted Feeling and Life.

This piece is one of a series of Angelic Upgrade books that fill you with Divine Angelic codes. Angelic laws are based on love and light and thus, operate for free-will, so we must call and ask the Archangels for help.

When working with your book relax, take deep breaths and ground to Mother Earth. Focus on Intentions for whatever it is your heart desires that are for the highest good of all involved. Intentions for these energies that we can not see but feel when we are ready. There are those that believe The Archangels are the Ones that make Law of Attraction Work.

This series of books take on a life of its own as the Archangels move and play from book to book, creating a Delicious Alchemy. Each book becomes an instrument in this Celestial Symphony for a more fulfilling life. Many of the Archangel books also carry and infuse the Violet Flame and Divine Connection to Mother Earth for a transformational experience.

Each book has a matching meditation audio available for your listening pleasure at https://archangelology.com. Please visit our site for your gifts. The book and the audio have similar wording, yet according to the Angels, they Upgrade us differently. Each medium has a unique experience, energetically Upgrading us in distinct ways. Each time you read or hear an Archangel Upgrade, a new dimension is added or adjusted for your benefit.

Become interactive with your book; when inspired, read the words aloud, and let them roll over you, feeling the love and magic that the Angels radiate. When inspired create your own rituals; there is no right or wrong way. As you play with the rock stars of the Celestial realm, you can expect your life to become more heavenly, more peaceful.

You may Notice Many Words are Uniquely Capitalized throughout this series; this is yet another way the Angels infuse us. When you see this try to feel that word or phrase; sensing the depth of its Intensity of Pure Divine Light throughout your Being.

The Archangel Energy is neither male

nor female. This gender fluidity is made clear in this series by the use of the word they or he/she speak to convey a non-gender energy that shifts roles to uplift and nurture you. The upgrades happen in Divine Time, and there is no schedule. There is no competition. There is no rush. Wherever you are in the process is perfect.

A word about the length of this book. "Less is more." This Series of books is the result of decades of study in the art of Law of Attraction, Angelic knowing and energy healing, condensed here for you in a format that will shift and benefit the reader. If you found your way here, you can expect miracles. As Einstein said, "There are only two ways to live your life. One is as though nothing is a miracle. The other is as though everything is a miracle." The matching audio to this book is 44 minutes, so working with that is always an option.

Both Neville Goddard and Albert Einstein stated that our imagination is the creative force. Goddard went so far as to imply that our imagination is the God/dess Energy. I mention this to you because as you read these words with much more than your eyes, let your imagination run wild with vivid pictures of the love the magical Archangels have for you and of your adventures together. Enjoy.

5

MARY MAGDALENE FEMININE DIVINE

Archangelology, Mary Magdalene, The Feminine Divine, Deep healing Breath. The Archangels have come to this very Blessed Divine Moment to help us play with the Feminine Divine Energies Infusing the planet Now. This Energy is lifting and bringing Light, Love, Hope, and the Feminine Archangels, Mary Magdalene, and many other Divine Beings, who want to Infuse us with this. This lovely moment, this present, this gift, this present moment with the delicious, empowering, joyful Energy that is the Feminine Divine - Deep Healing Breath.

Now, the Archangels want to remind us that their Energy is neither just feminine nor masculine. It is both swirled and combined with the Divine God/dess Energy that becomes the Divine Archangel Energy. Yet, for our game today, the Archangels will appear to us as the Feminine Divine, as female—deep Refreshing Breath.

The Archangels want to remind us that each individual, each person, is neither just female nor male Energy, yet the culmination of these energies. So now, at this time, we allow this Divine Feminine Strength to flow with a little more Ease with a bit more Grace with the intention of enhancing our lives in Beautiful, Joyful, Blissful, Sublime Ways: Deep, Invigorating Breath.

Stand with the Feminine Archangels now, and as you look around, see and feel a brilliant panoramic screen that flows around you in a circle. This screen is so lifelike that you'll smell, hear, and feel so happy and blissful. Feel it, yes, Deep, Nurturing Breath.

Know now that the Divine Feminine

Archangel Michael is standing by your side. She floats down with such Presence and Ease, and you feel this Magnificent Divine Angelic Being standing beside you and infusing you with Security, Support, and Serenity as you gaze upon this glorious site of Archangel Michael in her Feminine Essence. She reminds you that we will be activating the Divine Power of our imagination. She asks you to see her in all her feminine radiance, in all of her feminine Grace, and feel as she enwraps you in an energetic hug that makes you feel safe and protected. You experience her now as a warm embrace and know, on deep levels, how secure and protected you are in these Feminine Divine Energies. You may think about and feel this Mother Goddess Energy at any moment to activate your imagination creation to bring more sweetness and flow to your life. And you smile this Sweet "Inner Smile", that "Inner Smile" that you may activate at any moment, regardless of what is going on around you. And you may turn on that inner Secret Smile, and as you turn on that inner smile, your world Lights up around you. Yes, Deep Radiant Breath.

Now, as this is happening, the Divine Magnificent Mary Magdalene stands right with you, and you feel her Divine Presence; you feel her Royal Presence, her regality, her Divine Royalty. She stands Smiling with you, reminding you again of your Divine "Inner Smile", the Power of your "Inner Smile". Yes, Above Mary's head is a Glowing Golden Light, and you stare at it with awe and admiration. You feel as this same light emanates above your head like a Crown as Mary Magdalene reminds you that you are a Divine Being, the Divine Essence of the Divine Feminine—yes, Deep, Refreshing Breath.

******** "Inner Sweet Smile" Activation. Please take this moment to Pause. Take a deep, relaxing breath, and visualize Mary Magdalene standing before you. Allow her beautiful, Divine Feminine Energy to infuse you with deep Peace as Mary Magdalene guides you to activate your heart center. Call Archangel Haniel to assist while you take as much time as needed to feel all the Love in your Heart radiating in and around you. Breathe in deep Love, as you breathe out, fill your space up with all this Divine Love. Breathe Love in and out, and when ready, connect with your higher self. Archangel Raziel, the great Archangel of wisdom, stands beside you to help you feel your Higher Self coming online. Be easy on yourself, and know that your intentions for connecting with your Higher Self are making it happen. Feel as your Heart and Mind sync and align Together. Now, when ready, send your grounding cord down into Mother Earth and feel securely connected. Archangel Sandalphon stands beside you, helping you connect to Mother Earth now. Take your time, and when ready, feel your Violet Flame form a circle around you to establish healthy transmutative boundaries. Allow any non-beneficial or dense energies transmute to Love, Light, and Blessings. Archangel Zadkiel stands on your borders, helping you to run your Violet Flame in this Divine Feminine Circle. Hold this feeling as long as desired and allow your imaginative Feminine Energies to infuse your experience with Power and Peace. Feel and immerse yourself in this Divine Feminine Flow now.********

There are so many Benevolent Beings that want to be with you and support you. Mary Magdalene reminds you that you may call on these unseen Celestial Strengths any moment you choose. You may do this with yourself quietly, and no one else has to know how you can fill a room, a home, a neighborhood with light and fill the world, the universe, and galaxies with this Divine Golden Light. When activated, this Divine Golden Feminine Light brings Peace, Love, and Joy, so many things that, as humans, we love and enjoy—yes, Deep, Creative Breath.

The Archangels are so excited to be with us at this moment. When we say the word Peace, an Archangel gently floats in. She is Archangel Uriel, the Princess of Peace. Archangel Uriel, Deep Peaceful Breath. Archangel Uriel wants to remind us that we may call her to go before us, walk beside us, support us, and bring more Peace into our lives, and we may Shine this Feminine Divine Peace everywhere we go. We may Shine it in our Hearts; speaking of hearts, Mary Magdalene wants us to walk and float into an extraordinary place. When ready, we may align and go into our Heart Space. She expertly clears all pathways to Peace for you with the Grace and Ease of an Angelic Being. She gently infuses you with Angelic Frequencies of Peace as Angelic Relaxation fills your Mind, Body, Energetic Body, and Spirit on Angelic Levels.

Now, envision your Heart with me and go to your Heart's door. Remember, we will be activating our powerful imagination Now. Our Archangels are supporting us now, and we will walk into the heart space—deep Loving Breath.

Now, your Heart Space is the most beautiful Divine Place ever imagined. How does it look to you? Are there Vibrant Sparkles of Lovelight everywhere? Is there translucent Golden Light Shimmering? Visualize the most comfortable, relaxing place you have ever felt. As Mary Magdalene invites you into your Heart Space, she wants to give you gifts. She wants to give you a magical piece of Citrine to hold and feel. Mary wants you to know that this Citrine Gemstone Energy fills you with Bliss when you need a lift, more Happiness, and a sense of Abundance. She wants you to know that you will be lifted and guided with this Citrine and the Mary Magdaline, Mother Mary, Feminine Divine Energy—deep healing Breath.

As you take this Citrine, you may feel it as a beautiful Angelic Frequency of Sparkling Jewels. As you receive this gift, you feel the Love and the Peace, and you Smile, and again your Inner Smile Ignites.

******** "Inner Sweet Smile" Activation. Please take this moment to Pause. Take a deep, relaxing breath, and visualize Mary Magdalene standing before you. Allow her beautiful, Divine Feminine Energy to infuse you with deep Peace as Mary Magdalene guides you to activate your heart center. Call Archangel Haniel to assist while you take as much time as needed to feel all the Love in your Heart radiating in and around you. Breathe in deep Love, as you breathe out, fill your space up with all this Divine Love. Breathe Love in and out, and when ready, connect with your higher self. Archangel Raziel, the great Archangel of wisdom, stands beside you to help you feel your Higher Self coming online. Be easy on yourself, and know that your intentions for connecting with your Higher Self are making it happen. Feel as your Heart and Mind sync and align Together. Now, when ready, send your grounding cord down into Mother Earth and feel securely connected. Archangel Sandalphon stands beside you, helping you connect to Mother Earth now. Take your time, and when ready, feel your Violet Flame form a circle around you to establish healthy transmutative boundaries. Allow any non-beneficial or dense energies transmute to Love, Light, and Blessings. Archangel Zadkiel stands on your borders, helping you to run your Violet Flame in this Divine Feminine Circle. Hold this feeling as long as desired and allow your imaginative Feminine Energies to infuse your experience with Power and Peace. Feel and immerse yourself in this Divine Feminine Flow now.********

Yes, now another Beautiful Archangel wants to float into our Heart Space, where we are so peaceful and enjoying ourselves. She is the Divine, Radiant Archangel of the Violet

Flame Archangel Zadkiel. Archangel Zadkiel wants to give you this gift of the Violet Flame, and she reminds you of your ability to Radiate Violet Flame from your Heart. She passes you a vibrant piece of Amethyst. She reminds you of your ability to Activate your Divine Feminine Violet Flame as your Divine Feminine Violet Flame starts radiating all around you and throughout your Heart Space, Deep Refreshing Breath.

Your Heart Space Feels so Divine, and you can see shimmering traces of Violet Light, yes, Deep, Vibrant Breath. You gaze upon the Glorious Archangel Zadkiel, and she is smiling at you, reminding you of all the Everlasting Divine Love shimmering upon you now as you feel your Blessings from all the Archangels.

The Divine Mary Magdalene and Mother Mary want to come to join our party. In floats the Divine, Elegant Mother Mary—deep Nurturing Breath. Mother Mary floats to you and places a Shimmering White Diamond Light in your aura and Heart Space, radiating like a billion diamonds. And the beautiful Feminine Archangel Zadkiel infuses you with Forgiveness; take a deep self-love breath. She reminds you to let it all go. Let anything that no longer serves you go, and allow Divine Feminine Loving Forgiveness to infuse you - to infuse every cell of your energetic, emotional, and physical bodies, and to feel this Divine Feminine Forgiveness and what a gift it is in the Present moment. As she does this, the Divine Feminine Zadkiel continues to Infuse you with the Divine Feminine Violet Flame and her beautiful Forgiveness Energies. She is the Archangel of Forgiveness and signals to you telepathically to Activate your Inner Sweet Smile.

******** "Inner Sweet Smile" Activation. Please take this moment to Pause. Take a deep, relaxing breath, and visualize Mary Magdalene standing before you. Allow her beautiful, Divine Feminine Energy to infuse you with deep Peace as Mary Magdalene guides you to activate your heart center. Call Archangel Haniel to assist while you take as much time as needed to feel all the Love in your Heart radiating in and around you. Breathe in deep Love, as you breathe out, fill your space up with all this Divine Love.

Breathe Love in and out, and when ready, connect with your higher self. Archangel Raziel, the great Archangel of wisdom, stands beside you to help you feel your Higher Self coming online. Be easy on yourself, and know that your intentions for connecting with your Higher Self are making it happen. Feel as your Heart and Mind sync and align Together. Now, when ready, send your grounding cord down into Mother Earth and feel securely connected. Archangel Sandalphon stands beside you, helping you connect to Mother Earth now. Take your time, and when ready, feel your Violet Flame form a circle around you to establish healthy transmutative boundaries. Allow any non-beneficial or dense energies transmute to Love, Light, and Blessings. Archangel Zadkiel stands on your borders, helping you to run your Violet Flame in this Divine Feminine Circle. Hold this feeling as long as desired and allow your imaginative Feminine Energies to infuse your experience with Power and Peace. Feel and immerse yourself in this Divine Feminine Flow now.********

Now, as we stand with this Self Love

Forgiving Energy, we feel the Energies of the Divine Feminine Archangel Metatron Float gently into our Heart Space. Ah, feel the Golden tingles.

Archangel Metatron is the Feminine Divine Archangel of Sacred Geometry, so now we create with Golden Empowering Sacred Geometry. We experience invigorating shapes and can see Sacred Geometric Golden patterns moving around our Hearts. Feel Your Feminine Divine Power in this Now. You are Magnificent. Ask Archangel Metatron to Ground you now. Feel as your energetic roots connect deep in the earth now. Let your connection to Mother Earth, the Ultimate Feminine Divine Energy, Empower you.

See a glorious six-pointed star moving around, slowly spinning-- spinning at the speed you feel is the best for you in the moment, in the Powerful Now. Align as this Divine Feminine Star Sparkles. This Star of Light. This Star of Love. This Star of Freedom. This Star of Peace. This Star of so many Divine Frequencies on which we Thrive. Downloads of Bliss, Love, Peace, Freedom, and Happiness. These Glorious Energetic Downloads of Sacred Geometry, Feminine Divine Light Codes, and Angelic Frequencies become infused into our Forgiveness Freedom Energy as Forgiveness brings more Freedom. Freedom by creating more Divine Energetic Space with the Superpower Divine Feminine Energy. With the Grace and Ease of Bliss, it feels like joy; yes, take a Deep, Freeing Breath. This Divine Feminine Download feels like Forgiveness, Happiness, Love, and light as we take a deep, freeing breath. When we say "Superpower," a very special Divine Feminine Energy is activated—our Superpower Saints Frequency. Let us now call Saint Lucy, Saint Martha, and Saint Rita to join this Divine Feminine Freedom Creation. Saint Lucy stands beside you to infuse Divine Feminine Sacred Geometry with the gift of Intuitive Sight. Saint Lucy sparkles your third eye with the energetic ability to "see" which way to go for a more fulfilling life. Now, Saint Rita, the Saint of "wishes," shimmers with Divine Golden light in mesmerizing Sacred Geometry patterns to fill your life with more Blessings. Now, Saint

Martha steps forward, the powerful protector of women and children. Saint Martha enfolds you in a Brilliant fiery wall of Energetic Protection.

Relax and enjoy as these Three Feminine Divine Saints join to infuse you with Frequencies of Divine Freedom. Feel Divine Feminine Power that Lifts and Empowers you anytime you call them. Feel this Celestial Trinity of Divine Radiance, Enlivening and Prospering your Energy. Feel how Fortunate you are now. Feel Divine Feminine Freedom infused in your cells and Mind. Feel as your cells light up with Angelic Light Codes. Be that which you seek with this Celestial Support. Feel it all around you, relaxing and reminding you they have your back. You have a huge support team. You can relax into more Self-Love and Peace now as these Benevolent Beings lead you in a new Divine Feminine Way that evolves with and for you. Archangel Metatron wants to remind you that she will bring Her Sacred Geometry Light Codes to you anytime you desire. For any situation you would like a little Angelic Magic with, she will work this

Angelic Sacred Geometry throughout your Life and Spirit.

All you need to do is call. All we need to do is call any of the Archangels or Super-power Saints (who all have their book and audio at archangelologydotcom) to help you, be with you, and bring Their Divine Feminine Energies into your Heart and life. All these Benevolent Beings are with you in their Divine Feminine Form, helping you to visualize Happiness and helping you feel joy. Take a Divine moment now to Activate your Inner Sweet Smile.

******** "Inner Sweet Smile" Activation. Please take this moment to Pause. Take a deep, relaxing breath, and visualize Mary Magdalene standing before you. Allow her beautiful, Divine Feminine Energy to infuse you with deep Peace as Mary Magdalene guides you to activate your heart center. Call Archangel Haniel to assist while you take as much time as needed to feel all the Love in your Heart radiating in and around you. Breathe in deep Love, as you breathe out, fill your space up with all this Divine Love. Breathe Love in and out, and when ready, connect with your higher self. Archangel Raziel, the great Archangel of wisdom, stands beside you to help you feel your Higher Self coming online. Be easy on yourself, and know that your intentions for connecting with your Higher Self are making it happen. Feel as your Heart and Mind sync and align Together. Now, when ready, send your grounding cord down into Mother Earth and feel securely connected. Archangel Sandalphon stands beside you, helping you connect to Mother Earth now. Take your time, and when ready, feel your Violet Flame form a circle around you to establish healthy transmutative boundaries. Allow any non-beneficial or dense energies transmute to Love, Light, and Blessings. Archangel Zadkiel stands on your borders, helping you to run your Violet Flame in this Divine Feminine Circle. Hold this feeling as long as desired and allow your imaginative Feminine Energies to infuse your experience with Power and Peace. Feel and immerse yourself in this Divine Feminine Flow now.********

Now Archangel Raphael floats in her Divine Beauty. She looks so strong, Vibrant, and Abundant; she radiates a Divine Emerald Green Light and feels so luxurious. She feels to you like Fortune. She encourages you to feel your Abundance. Just seeing her sparkles, you feel so Powerful. You feel so Fortunate. Archangel Raphael wants to remind you not to get too caught up in "reality," yet to get much more wrapped up in visions of things that bring Peace, Prosperity, Love, and Happiness. Get wrapped up in your delicious imagination and get more wrapped up in the fabulous coming attractions. Take a Deep Abundant Breath- in Faith in Hope, and with the word Hope, we activate and feel as the Divine Feminine Archangel Gabriel gently floats in. Gabriel is the Archangel of Hope, Creativity, and Divine Faith. Understanding that Faith is the art of seeing the unseen - Deep Refreshing Breath and feel as Archangel Gabriel places her hand on your back and feel the tingles and the soothing as she touches you and your energetic body. Feel as Hope infuses you, and as you start to see visions of the life you dreamed of - of the life you dreamed of as a child, yes, feel that feel safety as all your

Archangels surround you and let you know it is safe. Now, it is safe to see the dreams that you desire; you're in a safe place. Saint Rita joins us to bring her gift of Divine Feminine Wishes and to let you know it is safe and fun to think about these dreams, and we don't have to attach to any of these visions. One can enjoy these visions and relish how good it feels to enjoy these dreams- the satisfaction that comes with these beautiful dreams. Yes, Deep Relieving Breath, and as we take that deep fortifying Breath, there is a smell of Sweet Divine Roses, the smell of high Vibration and Frequency as your vibration lifts. As your vibration lifts as Mother Mary and Mary Magdalene Smile their Inner Sweet Secret Smile, start to smile your Inner Sweet Secret Smile as you hold these visions with Peace with Harmony.

******** "Inner Sweet Smile" Activation. Please take this moment to Pause. Take a deep, relaxing breath, and visualize Mary Magdalene standing before you. Allow her beautiful, Divine Feminine Energy to infuse you with deep Peace as Mary Magdalene guides you to activate your heart center. Call

Archangel Haniel to assist while you take as much time as needed to feel all the Love in your Heart radiating in and around you. Breathe in deep Love, as you breathe out, fill your space up with all this Divine Love. Breathe Love in and out, and when ready, connect with your higher self. Archangel Raziel, the great Archangel of wisdom, stands beside you to help you feel your Higher Self coming online. Be easy on yourself, and know that your intentions for connecting with your Higher Self are making it happen. Feel as your Heart and Mind sync and align Together. Now, when ready, send your grounding cord down into Mother Earth and feel securely connected. Archangel Sandalphon stands beside you, helping you connect to Mother Earth now. Take your time, and when ready, feel your Violet Flame form a circle around you to establish healthy transmutative boundaries. Allow any non-beneficial or dense energies transmute to Love, Light, and Blessings. Archangel Zadkiel stands on your borders, helping you to run your Violet Flame in this Divine Feminine Circle. Hold this feeling as long as desired and allow your imaginative Feminine Energies to infuse your experience with Power and Peace. Feel and immerse yourself in this Divine Feminine Flow now.********

As this happens, feel as another Divine Archangel floats down, this is Archangel Sandalphon. She is the Archangel of Heavenly Harmony; she brings more Harmony into your life. She connects us with Source Energy. While holding these magnificent visions, feel as a tube of delicious white diamond light forms around your entire energetic body. This Angelic Light Frequency tube goes all the way up to the heavens, and feel that Divine Connection to the God/dess Energy, and feel as Archangel Sandalphon helps you to hum and get in a joyful place. Hum with your Archangel now. Hum and feel all these Archangels around you. You may hum aloud anytime you want to lift your Vibration. Humming is also excellent for relaxing, so practice when needed. Now relax as Archangel Sandalphon vibrates your beautiful blue throat chakra and see the Divine Female Archangel Michael standing beside you as well. You are now safe to express your throat chakra and take a Deep Refreshing Breath as Archangel Samdalphon and Archangel Michael stand in their Divine Feminine Glory. They help you hum and express 'yes,' feel that Divine Energy that allows your voice to express. Express the Divine Feminine Angelic Frequencies. The Divine Feminine sits back and is a Masterful Eloquent Frequency feeling. She can take action in her own sweet time in her Mind, Heart, and energetic body. She does not have to take action until she knows that it is the Divine Feminine Intuition. Feel the Divine Feminine Intuition as your soothing light tube connects you to the Divine Feminine Goddess Energies. As you connect back with your Goddess energies, you evolve with these energies.

Speaking of connection in floats, Archangel Raziel, with her Divine Feminine Angelic Wisdom. Archangel Raziel is the perfect Archangel to play with when you want to call in the other Archangels. Call her when you want to play with your Divine Feminine Wisdom, and she will float in. She is so Magnificent, with her Divine Secret

Smile, and you feel and see how wise she is. Let's ask now, Archangel Raziel, Divine Archangel of Knowledge and Wisdom: please infuse me with your wisdom, and you smile your "Secret Smile." You delight as Archangel Raziel surrounds you with Shimmering Diamond light, aligning your third eye with

Wisdom and Power; feel and smell brilliant tulips. We ask that only what is for our highest good comes to us with this energetic wisdom, with Grace and Ease, at a lovely, perfect pace of Divine Feminine Energy. There is no hurry, no rush, as we enjoy the moment. This present is a gift.

******** "Inner Sweet Smile" Activation. Please take this moment to Pause. Take a deep, relaxing breath, and visualize Mary Magdalene standing before you. Allow her beautiful, Divine Feminine Energy to infuse you with deep Peace as Mary Magdalene guides you to activate your heart center. Call Archangel Haniel to assist while you take as much time as needed to feel all the Love in your Heart radiating in and around you. Breathe in deep Love, as you breathe out, fill your space up with all this Divine Love.

Breathe Love in and out, and when ready, connect with your higher self. Archangel Raziel, the great Archangel of wisdom, stands beside you to help you feel your Higher Self coming online. Be easy on yourself, and know that your intentions for connecting with your Higher Self are making it happen. Feel as your Heart and Mind sync and align Together. Now, when ready, send your grounding cord down into Mother Earth and feel securely connected. Archangel Sandalphon stands beside you, helping you connect to Mother Earth now. Take your time, and when ready, feel your Violet Flame form a circle around you to establish healthy transmutative boundaries. Allow any non-beneficial or dense energies transmute to Love, Light, and Blessings. Archangel Zadkiel stands on your borders, helping you to run your Violet Flame in this Divine Feminine Circle. Hold this feeling as long as desired and allow your imaginative Feminine Energies to infuse your experience with Power and Peace. Feel and immerse yourself in this Divine Feminine Flow now.********

Now the Princess of Peace Archangel

Uriel flutters her Magnificent Wings. As you feel this Divine Transmission, feel Cosmic Consciousness shimmering around you. The Divine Feminine Archangel Orion is floating gently down. Archangel Orion is the Female Archangel of Cosmic Consciousness. She is here now to help you Enlighten with Divine Cosmic Consciousness, and she looks so Powerful. You feel the Divine Archangel Orion smile her "Secret Smile" at you. Archangel Orion starts to infuse your Heart and Mind Area with an Infinity Sign in Gold, a beautiful sideways eight, imbuing you with another strong connection for more Heart-centered thinking connected to the Mind. You can Relax Now. Allow your Mind and Heart to sync for Heart-filled thinking. You can release any fears, anything that no longer serve you, and you can embrace your Power as a Magnificent Feminine Divine Earth Angel. Feel as your Earth Angel Etheric Wings Activate and shimmer Rainbow light colors behind you. Strength for Love, Power, Happiness, and Light. Golden Light Energy shimmers you, as Archangel Raphael supports you in this

Divine Knowing. Yes, Deep Harmonious Breath.

Now, a surprise being is floating down to you, floating with their wings, and you Smile your Secret Smile so big because right in front of you appears a beautiful Magnificent Female Pegasus. She is that Heavenly Female Figure with her White Golden Wings; the colors around her move, change, and refresh the Energy all around you. Feel the sparkles. Your Exquisite and familiar Pegasus comes closer to you and telepathically lets you know that it is alright now to activate your Etheric Feminine Archangel Wings, yes, Deep Restoring Breath. As you Activate these beautiful wings at your back, you feel them Radiate as you Vibrate a Feminine Divine Frequency. Your Feminine Divine Wings are as natural to you as breathing, deep, refreshing Breath. Your Pegasus asks if you would like to get on her back and ride with her because she wants to take you on a journey. You Smile that "Inner Sweet Smile," and you are ready. You float up onto your Pegasus with such Strength and Grace, and the two of you Fit Together Perfectly. You feel so Safe and Secure, and you feel as the Violet Flame Infuses you, as if you're moving together in Sync as One, and your Archangels are moving all around you with Mary Magdalene and Mother Mary. And who should appear beside you, the magnificent, radiant Archangel Haniel? She is the Divine Feminine Archangel of Love. You start to get so excited when you see her because she reminds you that "Together" the master Switchboard, thank you, James Megan, for those beautiful Switchboards, she reminds you that "Together" you are going to follow a Golden lit-up path to where you want to go, deep healing Breath. Archangel Haniel lets you know that when you ask your Pegasus, she, the Archangels, and Mary Magdalene will help you follow a beautiful yellow path, a golden path, a Fortunate path that lights up for you. A golden Abundant path to more Love, a golden Abundant path to more Happiness, a path to more joy, a path to more relaxation.

This path will lead you to more Joy. You feel yourself float and fly with such Grace and Confidence; you are like a Magnificent

7

ANGELIC HABITS

There is a saying that our habits make us who we are.

The habit of calling in our Angels creates more peace and poise. As we stop, take a deep breath and call our Angels, this is an opportunity to ground into the now moment and, if we are really on our game, also ground into our beautiful mother earth.

Calling our Angels takes practice and forethought it is a wonderful way to calm fear or anxiety. Acknowledging this Angelic Support allows us to see perceived "challenges" as opportunities. Reminding us that we are never alone and are supported by the

Goddess, with Goddess energy flowing through you. Please remember that it makes no difference whether you are female or male, because as this Goddess energy flows through you, it empowers you. The great King Solomon was well known for working with the Goddess Energies and obviously had wonderful results. As you flow this Goddess energy through with the intention of creating the Highest Good, Miracle Mindset for you and all involved, you can let go as this path lights up for you.

Feel as Archangel Haniel is floating beside you, take a deep healing breath as this Archangel supports you in Love and Alignment as you feel Rose Quartz sparkles all around you. Take a moment to experience Rose Quartz energy all around you. It feels phenomenal. You feel Divine, deep-healing Breath.

******** "Inner Sweet Smile" Activation. Please take this moment to Pause. Take a deep, relaxing breath, and visualize Mary Magdalene standing before you. Allow her beautiful, Divine Feminine Energy to infuse you with deep Peace as Mary Magdalene guides you to activate your heart center. Call Archangel Haniel to assist while you take as much time as needed to feel all the Love in your Heart radiating in and around you. Breathe in deep Love, as you breathe out, fill your space up with all this Divine Love. Breathe Love in and out, and when ready, connect with your higher self. Archangel Raziel, the great Archangel of wisdom, stands beside you to help you feel your Higher Self coming online. Be easy on yourself, and know that your intentions for connecting with your Higher Self are making it happen. Feel as your Heart and Mind sync and align Together. Now, when ready, send your grounding cord down into Mother Earth and feel securely connected. Archangel Sandalphon stands beside you, helping you connect to Mother Earth now. Take your time, and when ready, feel your Violet Flame form a circle around you to establish healthy transmutative boundaries. Allow any non-beneficial or dense energies transmute to Love, Light, and Blessings. Archangel Zadkiel stands on your borders, helping you to run your Violet Flame in this Divine Feminine

Circle. Hold this feeling as long as desired and allow your imaginative Feminine Energies to infuse your experience with Power and Peace. Feel and immerse yourself in this Divine Feminine Flow now.********

Feel and immerse yourself in this Divine Feminine Flow now. As you're floating and feeling your Magnificent Earth Angel Wings, another Archangel, in her Feminine Divine form, appears beside you. Here is Archangel Camael, and she wants you to know that anytime you call her, she is with you, she is with you shimmering Divine Courage and Confidence in your life, deep healing Breath. Now call by singing Archangel Camael, Archangel Camael, Archangel Camael, feel as Archangel Camael infuses your base chakra, that chakra at the base of your spine. She, in her Divine Feminine form, infuses you with

Confidence, with safety, with feeling safe, with knowing that you can call on her anytime, and her Divine Courageous Feminine Force will shimmer. She will shower your Heart, she will lead your Heart, and she will help you think with your Heart Space, with Courage, to share Love in every aspect of your life. She reminds you that as Archangel Haniel moves forward with you and you move forward with Archangel Camael, and as the three of you move forward Together on this beautiful Golden Light Path, you can even see Golden Light Abundance Coins. As you move forward, they want to remind you to have the Courage to remember that everything you want, everything you need, everything that is for your highest good, is being shown to you at just the right Divine Time. You look, and you see your beautiful Golden pathway lit up for you, so easy for you to follow, and as you feel the Might and Strength of your Divine Feminine Power as you are riding on your Pegasus. You feel this strength moving forward, moving forward in your life, deep healing Breath. You feel spiritual strength, this Love Strength, this Divine Strength, this Physical Strength. You feel this resilience with your Archangels and your Pegasus. You feel your Angel Wings shimmering with light, and you feel this infusion in every cell in your Mind, your Body, and your Spirit. You feel this

Divine Power in your Mitochondria in your genes, infusing your Heart, you feel the strength infusing your Mind to think from your Heart Space with Love — deep Loving Breath. You feel this Alignment, and you feel the Violet Flame. You remember that the Violet Flame is infusing you as well, to have Peace, yes, deep Peaceful Breath, and as you look upon your screen and you see Yourself and your Archangels and your Mary's infusing you and loving you. Feel the Divine Femine Flow now and you Smile that Secret Divine Feminine Smile Yes feel it press your tongue against the roof of your mouth and feel that beautiful inner smile just radiating out of you and feel the Divine Feminine and feel how this lights up Your World and know that just by Existing You Bring Lght and Love to the world thank you feel these lights, feel these Archangels, feel this Peace.

******** "Inner Sweet Smile" Activation. Please take this moment to Pause. Take a deep, relaxing breath, and visualize Mary Magdalene standing before you. Allow her beautiful, Divine Feminine Energy to infuse you with deep Peace as Mary Magdalene guides you to activate your heart center. Call Archangel Haniel to assist while you take as much time as needed to feel all the Love in your Heart radiating in and around you. Breathe in deep Love, as you breathe out, fill your space up with all this Divine Love. Breathe Love in and out, and when ready, connect with your higher self. Archangel Raziel, the great Archangel of wisdom, stands beside you to help you feel your Higher Self coming online. Be easy on yourself, and know that your intentions for connecting with your Higher Self are making it happen. Feel as your Heart and Mind sync and align Together. Now, when ready, send your grounding cord down into Mother Earth and feel securely connected. Archangel Sandalphon stands beside you, helping you connect to Mother Earth now. Take your time, and when ready, feel your Violet Flame form a circle around you to establish healthy transmutative boundaries. Allow any non-beneficial or dense energies transmute to Love, Light, and Blessings. Archangel Zadkiel stands on your borders, helping you to run your Violet Flame in this Divine Feminine

Circle. Hold this feeling as long as desired and allow your imaginative Feminine Energies to infuse your experience with Power and Peace. Feel and immerse yourself in this Divine Feminine Flow now.********

Now, beside you, another divine, beautiful Archangel appears in her Divine Feminine form. You see Archangel Barachiel: she is glowing a beautiful Diamond Light, a beautiful Rainbow Diamond Light, and she radiates so many colors. She telepathically reminds you that your Divine Feminine Power Secret Smile feels like Love, feel this in your Heart to count all your blessings in your Heart feel with me now all your blessings She reminds you that one of your most empowering gifts one of your most powerful knowings is when you are Loving- you are a Lover- when you Love you are Raising Your Vibration, smell the Roses, feel your Vibration Raise feel as Archangel Barachiel and all the Archangels help your Vibration to Raise yes count your blessings feel your Blessings see in your minds eye all your Blessings now feel how Blessed you are to have the Eyes to see this, see with your third eye. How you have the lungs to take deep breaths, feel the Love, feel the Love that you have for the Archangels and your Mary's. Feel as a tube that is around you goes deep into the Divine Mother Earth and feel your connection and feel all the Abundance that the Divine Feminine Mother Earth flows to us, and as we give Love to our Mother Earth, feel how she Blossoms in your Love, feel this — feel all your blessings "Barukh, another word for blessed like Barachiel. Feel all the Blessings from Mother Earth and feel all these Blessings infusing you through all time space through all dimensions and feel as your blessings are being infused all through your past all through your present and into your future — blessings throughout your future and knowing that everything will always be enhanced with your Secret Smile Feminine Divine — as you and your Pegasus float and you are infused with the crystaline Rainbow Light from the Goddess above, from the Divine Goddess Mother Earth from the Divine Feminine Archangels all around you and as this Divine Feminine Energy infuses you from every possible angle. Thank you, thank you, thank you, for being you, thank you Mother Mary, thank you Mary Magdalene, thank you Divine Feminine Archangels, thank you Heart Space thank you Heart Space thank you for this time Together, thank you for this infusion -this beautiful light infusion Together thank you for our Pegasus and our Violet Flame and feel "I am the Violet Flame in action I am the Violet Flame I am the light of Goddess Creation.

I am the Violet Flame, thank you.

6

YEAR OF THE FIRE HORSE AND YOUR PEGASUS

I brought in the matching audio to this book on the Feminine Divine over 4 years ago. I kept trying to get the matching book to manifest to no avail. Now, in the year 2026, the book comes rushing in. When I first discovered that 2026 is the Chinese astrological year of the Fire Horse, it dawned on me that this Feminine Divine offering has a Female Pegasus (another version of the Divine Horse Energies). I thought to myself, you can't make this stuff up. Please know that what you have in your hands is so beyond our human minds and that there is so much love for us here. The Archangels Divinely plan these teachings to Empower you in magnificent ways.

May this offering of this book and matching meditation audio on the Mary Magdalene Feminine Divine bring you blessings upon blessings

I send you peace and blessings

Kim Caldwell

Celestial Masters, the Archangels, and much more.

Make reminders for yourself in convenient places where you will see them stop, breathe and call your Angels.

Do you have an event coming up? Call your Angels now and let them line things up smoothly for you. Allow the Divine Intelligence of the universe to help you.

Please be patient with yourself and with your Angels. Let attachment to outcome go, and as they say, "go with the flow."

Please remember that Angels are on Divine Time, so let go of when you think things "should happen" and allow yourself to relax. Play with this and have fun just like you did as a kid. You can do it and enjoy the process.

We shall also be adding the habit of incorporating our “Secret Smile” daily for exponential results. Be easy on yourself and Love Your Life.

8

ANGELIC MANIFESTATION JOURNAL BONUS

Create more of the life you want with the Archangels as you explore and focus with your Angelic Journal. If you are ready, let's set intentions now to make your Book a Manifestation tool. It is said that humans have so many thoughts going on in our heads at once that it is hard for Angels and Spirit Guides to hear what we want help with. This is one of the many reasons it is so powerful to get very clear on what we desire and write it out in a designated journal for our Archangels. This way, they can understand our needs better and help us with our dreams and goals in Divine Time.

If it feels like there is a lot of repetition in

your Mary Magdalene journal ahead, please know that Esther Hicks, one of my favorite teachers, says, "Repetition is the best teacher."

It has been proven that when we write things down, more of what we desire comes to us. Goals get accomplished, and things flow with more ease. Adding the Amazing Archangels to your journaling just makes the results that much stronger. As we set intentions for what we want and take the time to focus and write it down in our journal, unseen forces move on our behalf. We are going to enlist the help of this Divine Knowing with our Archangel book in an interactive way and turn our book into a manifestation tool. We are also going to play with our books like children and have some fun. Children are powerful creators, and we will take on some of their great habits for their creative value.

Focus and underline ideas you resonate with in your book and become immersed in Upliftment. There is a deeper connection as we become interactive with our Archangel books. We may get colored pens and underline areas of our book that feel important or special to us. We may want to draw pictures of desired blessings or anything that makes us feel good. We may want to mark different areas of our book with hearts, stars, or Angel wings. Get sticky tab notes, a personal favorite, and stick them to your favorite pages you want to return to often. In your journal section, place a sticky tab on an area you want to let the Angels know to help you write in and as a personal reminder. Let your Angelic interaction and intuition guide you with what feels best. Neville Goddard and Albert Einstein both explained that our imagination is a creative force and can bring great blessings to our lives. We will bring our imagination fully into our process now. You may want to add stickers to enhance pages. Place a beautiful angel or magic looking card in your book as a bookmark. Get creative and give your book some personal character. Putting clover or flowers in your book to press and dry, adds some powerful nature magic to your process. Roses are a great choice as they have the highest vibration of any flower. You may give lovely flowers as an offering to your Archangels as well. Giving back is always a beneficial activity.

Everyone has magical abilities. Some of us know this, and some do not. My point is all these ideas are simple and will work for anyone who puts forth an effort and has the faith to relax and let go so the angels may do their work. Of course, anything we put out comes back to us, so we want to always include "for the highest good" in all requests.

In all my studies of magical herbs, cinnamon is found in many different traditions for enhancement of all things wanted and removing things not wanted. You may want to rub a dab of cinnamon mixed with a touch of olive oil on your journal in an intentional shape such as a heart for more love or the infinity symbol for more abundance. Then say to yourself, "I anoint my journal with success and happiness with the help of the Archangels." Anointment has been practiced for eons with much luck and advancement. Basil and Sage could just as easily be utilized. Anything that feels magical and speaks to you in your spice cabinet most likely has wonderful magical properties. Use these gifts of nature with intention and focus for a more joyous life. The idea is to create a magnet for all you desire that is for your highest good with your Archangel Journal.

You may want to underline ideas in colors that mean something to you. The sky is the limit, get creative and juicy with your book, knowing that amazing things are being created.

Next, we have dedicated pages that are waiting for you to fill them with your heart's desires that the Angels will help you achieve as long as they are for the highest good. You may write anything you want in your Archangel Journal. There is no right or wrong way to do this. You may ask the Archangels to help you release things from your life, share your hopes and dreams, or ask questions. I love to ask my angels questions and patiently wait to know they will lead me to the answer in Divine Time. Be open and honest with your journaling and the Archangels understanding that the only ones who need to see your Angel Journal are you and your Angels. Keeping your wishes to yourself is very powerful for manifesting as well.

We have created categories for you, and of course, there will Be freestyle areas, so play with this and have fun. After you play with your journal, you may put it away in a sacred space knowing all is in Divine Order. Remember, magic works just in its own time and asking where the results are will only block things, so relax, have faith, and patience. You may come back to read your Archangel book and add more to it at any time. Know that unseen beneficial forces are moving to help you now and forevermore. Play with and collect other Archangelology books and audios, remembering, "If you call them, they will come." Check out the Archangelology Archangel Journaling Book for more ideas on taking your Journaling Process to the next "celestial" level. The Archangels have tied this whole series Together for us in such a Divinely Intelligent way. Spend time in nature with your book, filling it with love, imagination, and Angelic magic for exponential results. You are a powerful creator and loved by all that is.

Write on the blank areas of your book and on the lined journal areas. Think outside of the box and let your kid like creative energies flow. Have fun, and add your own flair.

Please enjoy the process and expect wonderful things.

9

HEART ACTIVATION WITH ARCHANGEL HANIEL

Archangel Haniel has their own book and audio you may want to explore as you bring in the Heart Connection Portion of your Secret Smile. Here, let us journal any ideas we receive from Archangel Haniel on the best way for us to radiate Love with our hearts. Once you ask this Divinely Intelligent Love Angel how to connect to your Love and Heart, you might get messages in your dreams, during the day, or at another time when you are aligned and receiving. Please journal them here and build this area as you evolve. This is a process; enjoy the journey. The destination is simply loving yourself more, and that is each moment. Please relax about this whole process and have fun. Visualize your angel shimmering with technicolor shimmering pink and red hearts as you laugh and play together. Make this process your own. Connecting with your heart center is a personal experience, so grow with it here with your angel. Some days it will be easier than others. Welcome all aspects of yourself with more love.

10

ARCHANGEL RAZIEL HELPS CONNECT TO YOUR HIGHER SELF

Let us spend time journaling about the next step in our Secret Smile. We will connect to our Higher Self with the help of Archangel Raziel. Raziel is the Archangel of Wisdom. They are the perfect Archangel to help us connect with our Higher Self and merge it with our Heart Center. Intend for your Higher Self to come on more often, particularly when you are triggered. Your Higher Self is the part of you that is Divine Goddess Intelligence and your Birthright. Journal all the ways that Raziel suggests for you to connect. Visualize a beautiful, intelligent golden stream of consciousness coming from Raziels' third eye to your third eye (right between your physical eyes). Each person experiences their higher self uniquely. Setting your intention and calling your Angel gets the process going. Journal any feelings and Ideas you have about this process. Remember to connect your Higher Self with your Heart Love energy, blending the two. Take your time with this, and know that as you call your angels to help you while setting intentions for the Highest Good, wonderful alignment is happening.

11

ARCHANGEL SANDALPHON HELPS US GROUND WITH MOTHER EARTH

Our third step to our Secret Smile is to ground to Mother Earth. Call Archangel Sandalphon to help you do this and journal any unique ideas that arise. Feel Archangel Sandalphon guide you to send golden roots deep into the earth, as if you were a tree connecting to the Earth. Journal all the benefits you feel as you practice your grounding while radiating Love from your heart. Breathing Love in and Breathing Love out for as long as needed, then connecting to your higher self. Feel Sandalphon coaching you to align these 3 processes with more ease and grace. Let this process become second nature and turn it on anytime you want things to go more to your liking. Allow your power to come online, and let your Angels help you.

12

CALL IN THE VIOLET FLAME TO SURROUND YOU DURING YOUR SECRET SMILE

As you allow your Secret Smile to Bloom with your Archangels and Marys, there is a very transmutative power that arises from this alignment. Adding the Violet Flame in a circle around you brings a new level of Divinity to the Process. Visualize yourself radiating your Secret Smile while you're aligned with your Heart and Higher Self, grounded to the Earth, and encircled in the Violet Flame. You may choose to add the Violet Flame chant of "I am the Violet Flame in Action, I am the Violet Flame, I am I am I am I am I am the Violet Flame" to boost the benefits. Visualize Archangel Zadkiel assisting and running the Violet Flame all around you. Journal how good this feels and any revelations while practicing. Ask your Angels in writing to help with this.

13

MARY MAGIC AND ENERGY TRANSMUTATION

The Marys are filled with beautiful transmutative energy magic. Journal a list of any energy or situations in your life you would like your Archangels and the Marys to help transmute to something higher. Visualize Archangel Jophiel with their Glow abilities standing with the Marys around you, supporting you in the energy in your life, upgrading. Draw angel pictures of things shimmering and shifting to the best version of themselves to higher timelines. Mary Magdalene and Mother Mary carry deep Feminine Divine magic; call on them for help. Feel your power with your abilities to hold your Secret Smile and transmute energy with the help of these Divine Beings.

14

MARY MAGIC AND THE VIOLET FLAME ANGELS

Take a deep, slow breath and feel as the Violet Flame Angels appear beside you. On your other side, smile your Secret Smile as you feel the Divine Mary Magdalene and Mother Mary appear. Smile and visualize these magnificent Goddess-like beings shimmering you with Divine Feminine Energies, helping you feel loved and supported. List all the ways this Divine Mothering energy can assist you. Call upon these Divine Beings anytime you would like more Mothering support in your life. Visualize the sparkling, dynamic Violet Flame Angels dancing all around you, transmuting, healing

, and clearing the energy for the highest good miracle mindset.

15

CALL IN THE ARCHANGEL ORION FOR HIGHER CONSCIOUSNESS

As you radiate your Secret Smile, call Archangel Orion to help you see and understand how higher consciousness will benefit you and your life. Journal what messages you get from Archangel Orion and the ways you would like Orion to help enhance your life with higher thinking. Feels as Archangel Orion stands with you gently and patiently helping you connect to that part of you that is Divine and knows all. Journal any messages that come in for you. Allow this page to be filled with prayers and blessings for all the good in your life.

MORE HEART CENTERED IDEAS WITH ARCHANGEL URIEL AND MARY

Spend time with Archangel Uriel connecting to your Secret Smile and cultivating ideas that bring more love to you. Take time to journal anyone who gets you fully in your Love Energy when you think of them. Clear examples are babies and precious pets that, when we think about them, we automatically smile and feel love. If nothing like this comes to mind, no worries, ask the Archangels to help you think of ideas that bring you to this place of more love. Ask your Archangels to connect you to other lifetimes or timelines that fully align you with your Love Power. We do not have to see these timelines, just feel the love. Remember that your Love is your Power, and ask your Angels and the Marys to help you get and stay there more often, with greater ease.

16

ARCHANGEL CAMAEL CONNECTING TO YOUR HIGHER SELF

Connecting to our Higher Self takes courage. Who better to call for more courage than Archangel Camael? Visualize Archangel Camael standing on your right, Empowering you to connect with your Higher Self. Everyone experiences their Higher Self differently. You may feel like you get a deep sigh of relaxation, or you're floating on a cloud, when you connect to your Higher Self. Journal about how it feels and ask your Marys and Archangel Camael to help you align and connect now.

17

FEMININE DIVINE SAINT JOURNALING

Call the “Superpower Saints" a very special Divine Feminine Energy. Our Superpower Saints Frequency. Call Saint Lucy, Saint Martha, and Saint Rita to join this Divine Feminine Freedom Creation. Saint Lucy stands beside you to infuse Divine Feminine Energy with the gift of Intuitive Sight. Saint Martha sparkles your third eye with the energetic security to "see" which way to go for a more fulfilling life. Saint Rita, the Saint of "wishes," shimmers with Divine Golden light in mesmerizing Sacred Geometry patterns, filling your life with more Blessings. Journal about all the delightful fun you have with your Feminine Divine Saints here. Visualize these 3 Beautiful Feminine Saints in Technicolor, flowing and dancing around you as they Upgrade your Field.

18

FEMININE DIVINE SUPPORT AND ST. MARTHA

Saint Martha steps forward, the powerful protector of women and children. Saint Martha enfolds you in a Brilliant fiery wall of Energetic Protection.

Relax and Feel Divine Feminine Power that Lifts and Empowers you anytime you call. Feel Celestial Divine Radiance, Enlivening and Prospering your Energy. Feel how Fortunate you are now. Feel Divine Feminine Freedom infused in your cells and Mind. Feel as your cells light up with Angelic Light Codes. Be that which you seek with this Celestial Support. Feel it all around you, relaxing and reminding you they have your back. You have a huge support team. Journal all about your Divine Feminine team. Asking for help when needed.

St. Martha is a fierce protector. Visualize St. Martha walking with you and Mary Magdalene. See St. Martha in all her strong, gorgeous glory, moving her arms around you, shimmering Saint Magic to remove non-beneficial energies. Feel your secret smile as The Archangels join your Energetic Security Team. See, as your entire vision turns bright white, anything that's not beneficial drops or melts away. Allow Mary Magdalene, the Angels, and the Saints to fill those created spaces with Feminine Divine, Peace, Fortune, and Blessings upon Blessings. Journal all the ways these Divine Beings can help you.

19

BRING THE DIVINE FEMININE POWER IN FOR YOUR ANCESTORS

When we call our Ancestors for help, they will come. Ask Mary to help express gratitude for all the help your ancestors offer. Journal as you call in Mary Magdalene and Mother Mary to bring their gifts to your ancestral line. Clearing and healing it as the Divine Archangels come in and bring Angelic gifts to fill the spaces the Marys create with their Love Magic. This is a journey, so be easy with yourself and it, as always, enjoy.

20

HO'OPONOPONO TO CONNECT TO YOUR LOVE POWER

There are many times when it feels impossible to feel Love in our Hearts, or Love for ourselves, much less Love for others. This is where the Magical Practice of Ho'oponopono can help us. Ho'oponopono is the art of healing through love and forgiveness brought to us by the Ancient Hawaiian Culture. It is simple, and it works. When you can not feel love Be easy on yourself and Activate your Ho'oponopono. You do this by simply saying "I love you, please forgive me, I forgive you, thank you." Take time to get to a quiet place with your Journal and write that you are having trouble feeling that love from the Heart Center, which is your power, and call Archangel Zadkiel to assist with this. Archangel Zadkiels matching audio and book is filled with Ho'oponopono and Violet Flame to help you. All you need to do is put the part of you that can not feel love in a circle out in your field and send the Ho'o-ponopono to it by repeating the healing Ho'oponopono phrase "I love you, please forgive me, I forgive you, thank you" as many times as needed till you can feel a little more love. These parts of you that cannot feel love are welcome and deserve compassion, so Be very easy with them. You can also call your Marys, who are masters of Love, Forgiveness, and Compassion.

21

STAY IN YOUR LOVE POWER WITH ST BARBARA AND THE FEMININE DIVINE

Barbara is the Saint who helps with anger, making her an excellent choice to call on for our Secret Smile. Anger has its place and must be felt. Yet learning to swing out of anger into your Love Power Energy and activate your Secret Smile is invaluable for staying in your Divine Feminine Power. Please Be and Stay aware when "people" try to get you and keep you in anger and/or fear; they are not putting your best interests first. You must take back your Power and get in your Secret Smile energy once the anger has been expressed and felt. This takes practice, and you can do it. Call for your Divine Help and Connection. Visualize St. Barbara sending sparkles of white light to your third-eye area, right at your forehead, to help Activate your Secret Smile and create more Peace of mind and connection. Relax as Archangel Uriel stands with you, humming Divine Angelic Frequencies to support and lift you. Journal all the beautiful ideas flowing to you. Journal any anger "triggers" you would like Divine Help with and call your Marys for support. Stay in your Power, Earth Angel.

22

CONNECT WITH YOUR FEMININE DIVINE PEGASUS

Journal about all the Freedom and Joy you feel as you visualize riding on your Pegasus in pure bliss and freedom. This is an imaginative creation. Have fun with it and allow it to help you create more blessings in your life. What is your Pegasus name? What color are they? What do they love to help you with? Activate your childlike enthusiasm and creativity. Get out some colored pencils and draw all the wonderful things you and your Pegasus will create Together.

23

ACTIVATE YOUR EARTH ANGEL FEMININE DIVINE ANGEL WINGS

Throughout the Archangelology Meditation Audio and Matching Book Series, we are encouraged to allow our Etheric Earth Angel Wings to Emerge from our back. After all, you are an Earth Angel and your Earth Angel Wings carry much Divine Angelic Magic. Allow your Earth Angel wings to come online now. Journal how they look and feel. As we evolve and enlighten, there are times when we can get so into our Highest Self that we soar like an Angel above all the conditions and problems of the world, and gain a deep knowing that things will work out even better than we could have imagined. Journal about all the ways you can do this here creatively with Archangel Sandalphon, St. Rita, and the Marys. Feel your Power and Connection now and expound on it in your Journal.

24

JOURNALING MAGNETIC CONFIDENCE WITH ARCHANGEL CAMAEL

Call Archangel Camael and the Marys to shimmer more Divine Self-love and enhance Manetic Self-Confidence for you. You will be calling in Divine Feminine Alchemy at its best. You may visualize The Feminine Divine Energy Marys in a circle around you and Archangel Camael. Archangel Camael stands with her finger, shimmering with Pink Angelic Love Frequencies, to your Heart Area. Relax as you feel how loved and supported you are. Feel the Marys and Divine Angels bring more Magic and Miracles to your world. You may see the Violet Flame engulfing the scene as you relax into your well-being and the "Power of Now." Get creative with these Divine energies and have fun—Journal all your Magnetic Confidence.

25

CREATE FEMININE DIVINE "MAGICALS"

Charm a piece of Citrine, Rose Quartz, Coin, or any object you like with the Feminine Divine Energy. A Feminine Divine beauty oil would be lovely too. You may want to get your matching Mary Magdalene Audio available at Archangelologydotcom and listen as you hold your intended "magical" and ask that the Feminine Divine Archangels allow this piece to be a vessel to bring their Divine Feminine Energies to your life and help you remember to call on your Inner Sweet Smile more often. Get creative with this process. There is no perfect way. You may also hold your magical piece as you read the Sweet Smile Activation section with intention. Have fun and journal about all the different items you want to charge with your Feminine Divine Archangels, Saints, or Mary Magdalene. Bring your Feminine Divine into the physical. Be creative and have fun.

26

FEMININE DIVINE LIGHT CODES

Sacred Geometry, Feminine Divine Light Codes, and Angelic Frequencies become infused into our lives as we intentionally call them in for the Highest Good Miracle Mindset. We call for Freedom by creating more Divine Energetic Space with the Secret Smile Feminine Energy. With the Grace and Ease of Bliss, it feels like joy; yes, take a Deep, Freeing Breath. This Divine Feminine Download feels like Forgiveness, Happiness, Love, and light as we take a deep, freeing breath. When we say "Secret Smile," a very special Divine Feminine Energy is activated. Journal about all the Magical ways you intend this Divine Feminine Mary energy to Upgrade you and your life.

27

MARY MAGDALENE AND MOTHER MARY LOVE MAGIC UPGRADE

Our Powerful, Loving heart is our Power, and when we forget this and go into stories that do not serve us, we leave ourselves and our Goddess-Given Love Power. Call Mary Magdalene and Mother Mary to walk with you daily, everywhere you go. Journal all the places you would love for the Marys to go and spread Divine Love. You may send the Marys to anyplace you shop, to your home, to anyplace you can think of that you would like to Infuse with the Divine Feminine Love Power and enjoy over time, or immediately as these places become Magically Infused with the Feminine Divine Magic. Journal all the places in your world that you would like to send more magical Love. You carry a Regal Divine Frequency everywhere you go and can magically send it anywhere you choose. You are that Divine and Magical Earth Angel.

PLEASE WRITE A HELPFUL REVIEW

Please Be an Earth Angel and give a positive review if you enjoyed this book so others may find it as well. And may blessings come back for your help.

Thank you so much. May you always be Blessed and highly favored.

Kim

BLESSINGS

May the Divine Creative Force that Moves and Creates the Universes Bless and Enhance Every Wish You Ever Conceived that is for the Highest Good of All Involved. May Joy, Peace, and Purpose Be Yours all the Days of your Lives. Through All Time Space and Dimensions. So, Mote, it Be, and So It Is. I hope this book helps you in wonderful ways and radiates out to a gorgeous life for you and yours. May you always Be Blessed and Highly Favored.

May all Beings Be Happy and Free

Kim Caldwell, creator of the Archangelology Book and Audio Series

REFERENCES

Diana Cooper. The Archangel Guide to Ascension: 55 Steps to Light. (Hay House Inc.)

Esther and Jerry Hicks. The Essential Law of Attraction Collection. (Hay House).

Rose Manning. The Angels of Law of Attraction. (Rose Manning 2015).

Catherine Ponder. The Dynamic Laws of Prosperity. (Wilder Publications).

Elizabeth Clair Prophet. Violet Flame, To Heal Body, Mind & Soul. (Summit Publications, Inc, 1997)

Inna Segal. The Secret Language of Your Body. (Simon Schuster, Inc.).

James Mangan. The Secret of Perfect Living. (James Mangan)

Og Mandino. The God Memorandum. (Fell Publishers 1995).

MORE OFFERINGS

~

Visit https://archangelology.com to discover more Archangels and Super Power Saints

Each of the following books has a matching audio filled with healing music.

Archangelology Michael * Protection

Archangelology Raphael * Abundance

Archangelology Camael * Courage

Archangelology Gabriel * Hope

Archangelology Metatron * Well Being

Archangelology Uriel * Peace

Archangelology Haniel * Love

Archangelology Raziel * Wisdom

Archangelology Zadkiel * Forgiveness

Archangelology Jophiel * Glow

Archangelology Violet Flame * Oneness

Archangelology Sun Angels * Power

Archangelology Moon Angels * Magnetism

Archangelology Sandalphon * Harmony

Archangelology Orion * Expansion

Archangelology Blue Flame Angels * Freedom

The items below come in book only

Archangelology * Archangel Journaling

Archangelology * Archangel Breath-Tap Book

How Green Smoothies Saved My Life Book

Activate Your Abundance Book and Audio Program

The rest of the items below are available in Audio Format

Archangelology*Mary Magdalene*Feminine Divine Audio

Archangelology * Breath-Tap Super Power Saints Volume 1 Audio

Archangelology * Breath-Tap Super Power Saints Volume 2 Audio

Regeneration Meditations * Switchword Series with Solfeggio Frequencies audio

Radiating Divine Love * Switchword Series with Solfeggio Frequencies audio

Love Charm * Switchword Series with Solfeggio Frequencies audio

Dragon Sun Grounding Meditations * Cosmic Consciousness Series audios

Sweet Moon Sleep Meditation * Cosmic Consciousness Series

Enchanted Earth Sacred Geometry * Cosmic Consciousness Series audios

www.ingramcontent.com/pod-product-compliance
Lightning Source LLC
La Vergne TN
LVHW010101110826
845155LV00028B/439

* 9 7 8 1 9 4 7 2 8 4 4 5 6 *